Should Junk Food Be

BANNED

in Schools?

By Riley Lawrence

KidHaven
PUBLISHING

Published in 2018 by
KidHaven Publishing, an Imprint of Greenhaven Publishing, LLC
353 3rd Avenue
Suite 255
New York, NY 10010

Designer: Seth Hughes
Editor: Katie Kawa

Photo credits: Cover © istockphoto.com/AbbieImages; p. 5 (top) Peter Dazeley/Photographer's Choice/Getty Images; p. 5 (bottom) wavebreakmedia/Shutterstock.com; pp. 6, 7 (left and right) courtesy of the Library of Congress; p. 9 nano/E+/Getty Images; p. 11 Monkey Business Images/ Shutterstock.com; p. 13 BURGER/PHANIE/Canopy/Getty Images; p. 15 Africa Studio/ Shutterstock.com; p. 17 (top) Krylov1991/iStock/Thinkstock; p. 17 (bottom) margouillat photo/ Shutterstock.com; p. 19 Creatas/Thinkstock; p. 21 (notepad) ESB Professional/Shutterstock.com; p. 21 (markers) Kucher Serhii/Shutterstock.com; p. 21 (photo frame) FARBAI/iStock/Thinkstock; p. 21 (inset, left) Digital Vision./Photodisc/Thinkstock; p. 21 (inset, middle-left) Peter Gudella/ Shutterstock.com; p. 21 (inset, middle-right) Peter Cade/Iconica/Getty Images; p. 21 (inset, right) © istockphoto.com/DebbiSmirnoff.

Library of Congress Cataloging-in-Publication Data

Names: Lawrence, Riley, 1993- author.
Title: Should junk food be banned in schools? / Riley Lawrence.
Description: New York : KidHaven Publishing, [2018] | Series: Points of view
Identifiers: LCCN 2017035206| ISBN 9781534524828 (6 pack) | ISBN
  9781534524194 (library bound book) | ISBN 9781534524811 (pbk. book)
Subjects: LCSH: National school lunch program–Juvenile literature. | School
  children–Food–Government policy–United States–Juvenile literature. |
  Children–Nutrition–Government policy–United States–Juvenile
  literature. | Junk food–United States–Juvenile literature. | Food
  habits–United States–Juvenile literature.
Classification: LCC LB3479.U6 L39 2018 | DDC 371.7/160973–dc23
LC record available at https://lccn.loc.gov/2017035206
Printed in the United States of America

CPSIA compliance information: Batch #CW18KL: For further information contact Greenhaven Publishing LLC, New York, New York at 1-844-317-7404.

Please visit our website, www.greenhavenpublishing.com. For a free color catalog of all our high-quality books, call toll free 1-844-317-7404 or fax 1-844-317-7405.

CONTENTS

Personal Choice or
PUBLIC HEALTH?

Junk food, such as candy, cookies, potato chips, and soda, tastes good, but it's not good for the human body. This is why some people have made an effort to ban it from schools. They believe taking junk food out of schools will make students healthier.

Most people agree that it's important for kids to be healthy. However, some don't agree with the idea of banning junk food from schools. They think this choice should be made by students and their parents or **guardians**. What do you think? Read on to learn more about this issue before making up your mind.

Know the Facts!

Some people believe banning junk food from schools can help end childhood obesity, which is the state of being very overweight.

It's important to understand different points of view about issues such as junk food in schools before forming your own opinion.

POINTS OF VIEW

The **debate** over junk food in schools has gone on for many years, and people on both sides feel very strongly. In fact, even presidents have disagreed about banning junk food in schools!

When Barack Obama was president of the United States, the **U.S. Department of Agriculture** (USDA) announced a plan to take junk food out of U.S. schools. However, after Donald Trump became president in 2017, the new head of the USDA announced a plan to give schools more freedom over what they serve students for lunch.

Know the Facts!

Creating healthier school lunches was very important to First Lady Michelle Obama. She started the Let's Move! **initiative** to help fight childhood obesity.

Barack Obama and Donald Trump have different points of view about junk food in school lunches.

CONTROL

Should the government get to decide what you eat at lunchtime? That's a question asked by many people who oppose banning junk food in schools, and their answer is no. These people still want children to be healthy and want to fight childhood obesity. However, they feel it's not the government's place to tell schools, parents, and children how to do that.

Many people worry about the government having too much power over people's everyday lives. They think people should make their own choices, including the choice to eat junk food or healthy food.

Know the Facts!

In May 2017, it was announced that schools would be allowed to serve 1 percent fat flavored milk, such as chocolate milk, again instead of only fat-free milk. Also, schools wouldn't have to lower the amount of salt in the foods they served any more than they already had.

8

Many people who oppose banning junk food in schools think what kids eat should be decided only by parents and kids—not by the government.

A Public Health
PROBLEM

When health problems **affect** many people in a country, sometimes the government steps in to help. This is what happened in the fight against childhood obesity. Junk food has been banned in schools because people believe this will help make kids healthier, which makes the country healthier.

The World Health Organization (WHO) has called childhood obesity a public health problem. This means it affects the health of the whole population—not just in the United States, but also around the world. Banning junk food in schools has been seen as one way to improve public health.

Know the Facts!

Childhood obesity may cause many health problems as kids grow up, including heart problems, **diabetes**, and certain kinds of **cancer**.

Banning junk food in schools is one way to get students to eat healthier, and eating healthier is one way to fight obesity.

11

DIFFERENCE?

Some people believe a ban on junk food in schools is a key to fighting childhood obesity. Others, however, believe this kind of ban doesn't make much of a difference. They believe the real problem is what children eat at home and the amount of exercise they get each day.

It's also hard for healthy lunches to make a difference if kids throw them out. A 2015 study showed that kids were throwing away more fruits and vegetables than they were before lunches had to meet health standards.

Know the Facts!

A major study of junk food bans and childhood obesity was done in 2012. It showed that there was no link between schools that banned junk food and rates of childhood obesity among students.

Some people argue that schools are not where the problem with junk food needs to be addressed. Kids pick up their eating habits at home, which is where they often eat more junk food than they do at school.

HABITS

Students go to school to learn, and one of the things they learn about is how to be healthy. Some people believe banning junk food in schools helps kids learn more about healthy foods because that's all they see during the day.

When healthier foods are served in schools instead of junk, kids can be presented with new foods, such as turkey burgers and different fruits and vegetables. This can help them form healthier eating habits for their whole lives. They can even teach their parents about the healthier foods they eat at school.

Know the Facts!

In 2014, the U.S. government announced a plan to ban ads for junk foods from appearing in schools during the school day. This was done to help students make healthier choices.

Banning junk food forces many students to try new, healthier foods they may never have tried before. They may end up loving these healthy foods!

CHOICES

People who oppose junk food bans believe the best way to get students to learn healthy habits is by giving them the ability to make choices. They think banning junk food will only make it more appealing to kids because they can't have it.

Instead of banning junk food, they believe students should be given choices between healthy foods and unhealthy ones. Teaching students about good **nutrition** might then help them make healthier choices at lunchtime. Learning to make these choices on your own is an important part of growing up.

Know the Facts!

As of 2017, 20 percent of American children between the ages of 6 and 19 were considered obese.

Some people want to keep junk food in schools to **protect** students' right to choose what they eat. They believe teaching kids about healthy and unhealthy foods will help them make good choices.

OR

Junk on
THE BRAIN

Learning through making choices is important. However, some people argue that other kinds of learning **processes** are harmed when junk food is allowed in schools.

A 2014 study showed that students who ate more fast food were more likely to **perform** poorly on reading, math, and science tests. Fast food is like junk food because of its high amounts of fat, sugar, and salt. Scientists believe eating these kinds of foods often can harm a person's memory and can make it harder for them to learn.

Know the Facts!

Some studies have shown that children who struggle with obesity miss more days of school than other students.

People who want to ban junk food in schools believe it will help students perform better in the classroom.

DECIDE?

The problem of childhood obesity isn't going to be fixed by doing one thing, such as banning junk food in schools. However, some people believe getting rid of junk food in schools will play a big part in helping kids lead healthier lives. Others, though, think the choice of what kids eat should be left up to students and the adults who care for them.

After learning about the different points of view on junk food in schools, what do you think? Who should decide what you eat at school?

Know the Facts!

The Healthy, Hunger-Free Kids Act of 2010 set new nutrition standards in U.S. schools while Barack Obama was president. It was the first act in more than 30 years to have a major impact on the food served to students.

Should junk food be banned in schools?

YES

- Childhood obesity is a public health problem, and banning junk food could help children eat healthier.

- Banning junk food introduces students to healthier foods and eating habits.

- Eating too much junk food can cause students to perform poorly in class.

NO

- The government shouldn't decide what kids eat when they're at school.

- Taking away students' food choices keeps them from learning how to make healthy choices for themselves.

- Banning junk food in schools doesn't make a difference in obesity rates because kids can still eat junk food at home.

When deciding your point of view in a debate, it can be helpful to make a list such as this one to help you understand each side.

GLOSSARY

affect: To produce an effect on something.

cancer: A sometimes deadly sickness in which cells grow in a way they should not, often forming tumors that harm the body.

debate: An argument or discussion about an issue, generally between two sides.

diabetes: A sickness in which a person cannot properly control the amount of sugar in their blood.

guardian: A person who cares for another person.

initiative: An act or strategy to improve a situation.

nutrition: The method of eating the right kind of food so a person can grow and be healthy.

perform: To do something that requires a skill.

process: A series of actions or changes.

protect: To keep safe.

U.S. Department of Agriculture: A part of the U.S. government that is responsible for farming, forests, and food.

For More INFORMATION

WEBSITES

Healthy School Lunch Choices

kidshealth.org/en/teens/lunch-sheet.html?WT.ac=ctg

This simple set of charts can help you plan a healthy lunch and presents easy ways to make school lunches even healthier.

MyPlate Kids' Place

www.choosemyplate.gov/kids

The official USDA nutrition website includes facts about MyPlate nutrition guidelines, games, activities, and tips for living a healthier lifestyle.

BOOKS

Carole, Bonnie. *Junk Food, Yes or No*. Vero Beach, FL: Rourke Educational Media, 2016.

Etingoff, Kim. *Healthy Alternatives to Sweets and Snacks*. Philadelphia, PA: Mason Crest, 2014.

Lanser, Amanda. *School Lunches: Healthy Choices vs. Crowd Pleasers*. North Mankato, MN: Compass Point Books, 2015.

INDEX